CANADIAN ROCKY MOUNTAIN
NATIONAL PARKS

JOSEPH ALBINO

Front Cover Photo:
In front of the Banff Administration Building is Cascade
Gardens. The background view includes the town of
Banff and Cascade Mountain.

Back Cover Photo:
Yoho Valley Road

All Images Courtesy of
Ann Badjura
E-mail: abadjura@gmail.com

Except for pages 5, 9, 11, 12, 13, 16, 20, and front
cover photographed by Joseph Albino

To order additional copies of this book, contact:
Xlibris
1-888-795-4274
www.Xlibris.com
Orders@Xlibris.com

INTRODUCTION

During my youth, I developed a love for the great outdoors and for outdoor recreational activities initially as a Cub Scout and later as a Boy Scout with Troop 91 which was sponsored by Assumption Church in Syracuse, NY.

Under the tutelage of our Scoutmaster, Art Myers, along with dedicated committee members, I and my fellow Boy Scouts had the opportunity to spend many weekend camping trips all four seasons of the year in addition to two-week summer camping trips at Camp Woodland in Constantia, NY.

It was also during those years of Boy Scouting that I was introduced to the fabulous forests, lakes, mountains, rivers, and streams of the Adirondack State Park in northern New York.

During the summer of 1954, when I was a high school student, I had the opportunity to attend the Second National Boy Scout Jamboree which was held at Irvine Ranch in California.

Prior to the time of jet travel, I and my fellow Boy Scouts along with our Boy Scout Leaders traveled by train from New York to California.

One morning our train came to a stop in a western state which, if I recall correctly, was most likely Montana. I looked out the train window to see a hillside of stately evergreen trees and was told that we were near Yellowstone National Park. That was my first encounter with a national park.

Subsequent to returning from California, I earned the coveted Boy Scout Eagle award.

Now, as an adult, in my work as a professional writer-photographer, I have traveled throughout the United States and Canada. During my travels I have visited many national parks in both the United States and Canada and have photographed the parks, researched the parks, written about the parks, and published feature articles about the parks. I also continue my love of camping, canoeing, hiking, swimming, etc.

It is my hope that this picture book about the Canadian Rocky Mountain National Parks will be one more opportunity to share with you the reader my love of the great outdoors.

THE CANADIAN ROCKY MOUNTAIN NATIONAL PARKS ARE ONE OF THE SEVEN MOST POPULAR TOURIST SPOTS IN THE WORLD

By Joseph Albino

During the late 1800's, when the Canadian Pacific Railroad was building a cross-continental railroad from the Atlantic to the Pacific, three workers for the railroad discovered a natural hot springs at the base of Sulphur Mountain in what is today Banff, Alberta.

When the word of the hot springs became public, the three workers thought they could benefit from their discovery and tried to stake

legal claim. Numerous attempts to obtain ownership of the hot springs were made by others, so much so that in 1885 the Canadian government passed an order in council to protect the area and establish Canada's first National Park Reserve.

The natural hot springs became a special place belonging to all Canadians. By designating a 26 square km area around the hot springs as a reserve, it marked the beginning of the Canadian National Park System as we know it today.

One of the leaders of the Canadian Pacific Railroad saw a connection between the railroad, the hot springs, and the concept of a spa. He also concluded that if the beauty of the Rockies and pleasantness of the hot springs could not be exported to the people, perhaps the people could be brought to the hot springs.

Subsequently, the Canadian Pacific Railroad built the Banff Springs Hotel to house the tourists who would be attracted to the area.

The new hotel, combined with the birth of the National Park System and a continental rail line, led to the beginnings of modern tourism in Canada. The Cave and Basin National Historic Site within Banff National Park marks the location where the natural hot springs were first discovered.

The developers of the continental railway also built Chateau Lake Louise at Lake Louise plus Glacier House, which, in its day, was quite a place to stay, at Roger's Pass.

At that time, since Canada was part of the commonwealth, the developers wanted some focus on which to attract British tourists to the Canadian Rockies. Of note, in the early 1900's, Alpinism was very fashionable.

In fact, the first ascent of all the tallest mountains was taking place then, particularly between 1860 and 1890, especially by the well-to-do classes of the United Kingdom. Climbers in the Canadian Rockies had little or no experience in mountaineering, and many fatalities were the result.

Thus, the organizers of the Canadian Pacific Railway concluded if they were to bring professional guides from the Alps, guides that had experience in safely guiding their clients to the mountains, they would gain a certain clientele to frequent the newly built hotels. It was a smart plan, and it worked quite well.

The first guide the developers brought to the Canadian Rockies was Peter Sarbach who came from a small town called Sankt Niklaus which is near the well-known resort of Zermatt.

Subsequently, Canadian Pacific Railways brought over a number of guides between 1899 and the 1930's. These were Swiss guides who were based at the major hotels previously mentioned.

by author William Putnam in his book, *The Guiding Spirit*. Initially, the guides came over during the summer months and returned to Europe during the winter months. After about 1903, the guides tended to stay year-round.

These guides worked out what they considered to be the easiest routes to the summits of the major mountains in the Canadian Rockies. And after all these years, the original first ascent routes are still the established routes to the summits. Popular mountains included Mount Temple which is the highest mountain in the Lake Louise area.

Mt. Victoria, also in the Lake Louise area, was named after Queen Victoria. It forms the background panorama for the Chateau Lake Louise and is probably the most photographed mountain in the Rockies.

The mountains, and the guides who provided the guiding, attracted a number of tourists and left a legacy which has been captured

Mt. Lefroy, just east of Mt. Victoria, was named after an early observer of terrestrial magnetism. This mountain gained recognition after the death of Philip Stanley Abbot, the first mountain fatality in North America.

Mt. Assiniboine, which is considered the Matterhorn of the Canadian Rockies, is shaped like the Matterhorn. Mt. Assiniboine is named after an Indian tribe that lived in the Canadian prairies.

"Fifty Switzerlands in One" was one of the popular theme lines used in promoting the Canadian Rockies to the Victorian gentry. Many Europeans were familiar with the mountains of Switzerland. The idea was to indicate the Rockies were just as picturesque as the Swiss Alps but even more vast.

With the passing of time, three additional, adjacent National Parks came into existence. These include Yoho, Kootenay, and Jasper. Along with Banff, these four National Parks and three Provincial Parks (Mt. Assiniboine, Robson, and Hamber) in British Columbia comprise the **Canadian Rocky Mountain Parks World Heritage Site**, declared a World Heritage Site by UNESCO in 1984.

Canada's Rocky Mountain Parks are special places because of outstanding mountain ranges, lakes, rivers, forests, and wildlife, as well as the rich cultural and human history.

Visitors should stop initially at the Parks Canada Information Centre located in each of the mountain National Parks. For example, in Banff, the Information Centre is found in downtown Banff at 224 Banff Avenue.

Here, Parks Canada, the Banff / Lake Louise Tourism, and The Friends of Banff National Park provide information on Parks activities, accommodations, safety, etc.

The nature of today's tourist has changed dramatically. Visitors to the Parks aren't content to simply look at the Parks through the windows of an automobile, tour bus, or RV.

Instead, the tourist of today wants to understand the Parks in greater depth. The tourist wants to understand about the wildlife, ecosystems, geology and the history of the area. There are also tourists who want to know how a national park is managed, how it operates, and how to be a better tourist.

Rather than engage in passive sightseeing, more and more visitors to the four Mountain National Parks want to touch and feel the environment while engaging in sport and recreational activities

In that vein, there are, at this writing, more than 1,000 sport/recreational firms that are members of what is called the Banff-Lake Louise Tourism Bureau, and these firms offer a variety of soft adventures from backpacking to cross country skiing.

Visitors to the Parks who want to learn more about the Parks will have the opportunity to learn. In fact, many of the tour guides within the Parks are themselves biologists, naturalists, and scientists who can interpret the environment for the visitor, thereby increasing the enjoyment of the outing.

Today, visitors to the four Mountain National Parks enjoy a wide variety of activities all four seasons of the year while staying at an equally wide variety of accommodations, from campgrounds to bed and breakfasts to motels

bears and other hibernating animals begin to awaken, there are excellent wildlife watching opportunities for the visitor.

As the snow melts and the first green begins, creating what biologists call the salad buffet for

the wildlife, the bears become visible and create "bear jams" along the highways. Tourists pulling over in their vehicles to look at these wild animals in their natural habitat must remember to never approach, feed, entice or disturb any animals in the Canadian Rocky Mountain National Parks.

The Banff and Jasper town sites are also prime habitat for the elk that enjoy living in the valley just as much as the people do. In Banff alone there are more than 239 elk in the immediate town site area. In the spring, the elk are with their spring calves, with calving season running from early May until about the end of June.

and hotels.

Let's begin with spring when the mountains are coming alive with new growth. As the

Spring also marks the beginning of the fishing season, with outfitters available. With the return of the birds to the north country, bird watching is also a popular spring activity.

Of note, Wings Over The Rockies Bird Festival is held annually each May in the Columbia Valley adjacent to Kootenay National Park. The Festival features guided walks, river floats, and presentations that showcase area birds and wildlife.

The world famous 27-hole Fairmont Banff Springs Hotel golf course is a links-style golf course designed by Stanley Thompson who specialized in designing links-style golf courses similar to what are prevalent in Scotland.

Most tourists come to the Canadian Rockies because the National Parks provide an opportunity to hike on easily accessible trails, to engage in wildlife watching, to gain peace of mind in an out-of-door setting, and to see some of the best scenery in the world.

Golfing The typical destination golfer, based upon studies, would be a golfer visiting from eastern Canada, from the eastern seaboard of the United States, or from the southern United States including those trying to escape the heat of Florida, all coming to enjoy golf in the Canadian Rockies.

Golfing aficionados will appreciate that the master golf course architect, Stanley Thompson, was behind the courses in both Banff and Jasper. He designed the course at the Fairmont Jasper Park Lodge in 1925 and the course at the Fairmont Banff Springs Hotel in 1928.

Incidentally, it is believed the term links comes from the concept of links of sausages. The golf course is an out and in instead of a back and forth. In other words, the golfer heads out, loops around, and comes back.

Golf courses within the Rocky Mountain National Parks provide the golfer with the opportunity to view wildlife – bear, coyote, deer, elk – while golfing.

take escorted boat rides around the lakes. At Lake Minnewanka, one can take the boat ride to an area of the lake called Devil's Gap which is where the lake actually begins to make its way into the foothills of the Rockies. One can see where the Rocky Mountains taper off to the prairies.

At Jasper's Maligne Lake, the boat cruise makes a stop at Spirit Island which is one of the most recognized photographic views in the Canadian Rockies. Lake Minnewanka is the only lake in the Park on which motor boating is permitted.

Fishing Should a family want to engage in fishing on Lake Minnewanka, the same firm that rents motor boats also supplies licenses, tackle, rods, and other fishing gear. In both the communities of Banff and Jasper, there are firms that sell fly-fishing and fishing equipment. One can also rent fishing equipment from several stores.

Canoeing Canoes are available from concessionaires at Lake Louise, Moraine Lake, Maligne Lake, Emerald Lake, Pyramid Lake and within the Town of Banff. All the lakes are exquisitely attractive, and canoeing offers a relaxing opportunity to enjoy the lake vistas.

Guided Boat Rides At Maligne Lake and Lake Minnewanka, there are opportunities to

If a family wants to enjoy a private fishing trip, there are a number of firms that will supply guides by the day. The guide will pick up the family at the hotel/motel door, supply all the equipment, and take the family members for a fishing experience.

fish wanted, what was available that day, and Park regulations. The guides have access to the Bow and Athabasca Rivers and numerous alpine lakes.

Hiking Throughout the Parks, there are a multitude of short hikes. Many of them are self-guiding interpretive hikes which provide an opportunity for the hiker to learn about the environment he or she is walking through.

In Jasper a one to two hour hike will take one around the Old Fort Point Loop which provides a terrific view of the town of Jasper surrounded by a panorama of mountain peaks including snow-capped Mt. Edith Cavell, the tallest peak in the area.

The body of water the guide would be apt to take them to would depend on what the fishing was like at that time of year. The place to fish would be determined by the type of

Another popular hike in Jasper is Valley of the Five Lakes which can be done in 2-3 hours and is a popular family hike. The five small lakes are the highlights of this outing.

The hike begins with an easy walk through a forest of lodgepole pine then climbs across a flowery meadow to the lakes beyond.

In Banff, Johnston Canyon is a popular hike. The canyon features torrential waterfalls, interpretive displays, and paved trails that lead into the canyon. Trails have been constructed with handrails for the safety of the visitor.

Still another easy hike in Banff is the Marsh Trail. Below the Cave and Basin National Historic Site, one can take a self-guiding interpretive walk along the boardwalk constructed through the marshlands.

Another favorite in Banff is the Fenland Trail which takes the hiker around the marsh area of the Vermilion Lakes. Tranquil and scenic, the trail crosses through protected marshland and is also a self-guiding interpretive hike.

Paint Pots Trail in Kootenay National Park is a short trail that takes people to a colorful, cold water spring that has brought iron rich minerals to the surface and stained the soil yellow and red. This soil is called vermillion and was used for thousands of years by aboriginal peoples as paint for decorating their tepees, clothing, and bodies.

Lake Louise itself is considered the birthplace of recreational hiking in western Canada. It was the Canadian Pacific Railroad workers who discovered Lake Louise while working their way across the continent. They, in turn, also built trails from Lake Louise to the nearby scenic vistas.

Today, these same trails lead visitors into what many consider to be the most spectacular mountain scenery in all of North America. There are also more extensive hiking trails which would require, say, half a day or a full day to walk.

Some visitors equate Lake O'Hara to one of the prettiest places on earth. The area has all the attributes of a mountain environment. It is such a special and fragile place that a reservation system is in place to avoid

crowding and in turn preserve the natural environment. The quality of the visitor's experience is therefore maintained.

Heli Sightseeing Individuals and families can book helicopter trips to see the mountains from above instead of from below. However, sightseeing flights generally do not fly over the National Parks in order to help protect the ecological integrity of the area.

An operator will pick up the party at the hotel/motel and take them to Canmore, just east of Banff, where they would board the helicopter.

Children who take the helicopter ride are amazed by the scenery. Unless a family is going to engage in serious backcountry backpacking, they won't see the scenery they will see from the helicopter.

Camping There are numerous campgrounds for tents, travel trailers, and recreational vehicles. Indeed, camping is a very popular activity in the Canadian Rockies.

White Water Rafting At Banff, the firm that provides the ride will pick you up at your hotel, take you for a day of white water

rafting outside the National Parks, and bring you back to your hotel in the evening. Many firms also offer multi-day excursions. Unlike Banff, in Jasper there are a number of raft companies operating within the Park.

In Jasper there are several white water rafting companies that will take one on scenic trips down the Athabasca and Sunwapta Rivers. The river guides offer a range of experiences from wild to mild.

For those who want to avoid the risk of white water rafting, one can take a river float down the Bow River. In the absence of white water rapids, one has the opportunity to see wildlife along the river and learn about the area from an interpretive guide.

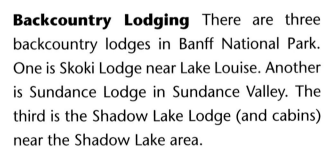

Backcountry Lodging There are three backcountry lodges in Banff National Park. One is Skoki Lodge near Lake Louise. Another is Sundance Lodge in Sundance Valley. The third is the Shadow Lake Lodge (and cabins) near the Shadow Lake area.

The backcountry lodging experience provides an opportunity for visitors to either backpack or, in some cases, horseback ride into these lodges and then to use the lodges as a hub in order backcountry areas.

All three backcountry lodges provide a different experience. Each backcountry package includes both accommodations and meals. The properties are both comfortable and environmentally sound.

Glacier Visit Driving the Icefields Parkway, from Lake Louise to Jasper, with a different scenic view at each corner, the visitor is in the area of eight large glaciers, three of them visible from the highway.

TAKALKAW FALLS

Takalkaw Falls is located in the
northeast section of Yoho National Park

photographed by Joseph Albino

The Canadian Rocky Mountain National Parks

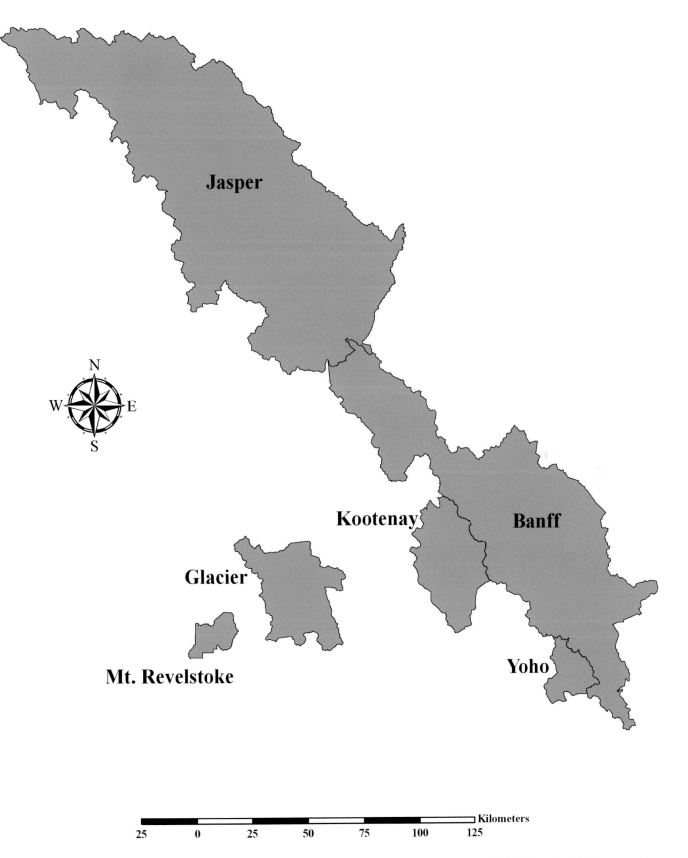

Jasper

Kootenay

Banff

Glacier

Mt. Revelstoke

Yoho

N
W E
S

Kilometers
25   0   25   50   75   100   125

© 2007 True North Cartographics

Across from the Icefield Visitor Centre, one can actually walk onto the Athabasca Glacier with an experienced guide or ride in comfort in a motorized snowcoach to an area where one can get off the coach to explore the Rockies' largest body of ice.

Jasper Walk Each evening, there is an opportunity to go on a walking tour of Jasper, the northern most community in the Canadian Rockies. In contrast to the Town of Banff, Jasper is the quieter of the two communities. Via Rail passes through Jasper and makes a stop there.

Hot Springs There are three fantastic Hot Spring Resorts located within the Canadian Rockies. Radium Hot Springs is located in Kootenay National Park; the second, Miette Hot Springs, is located due east of the community of Jasper; and the third, the Upper Hot Springs, is located north of the administration building in Banff.

September marks the beginning of the fall season. In the Parks, in the fall, visitors enjoy splendid weather, excellent hiking, and colorful foliage. The needle on the Alpine larch tree, a tamarack-like tree, turns a bright golden color in the fall.

There are some visitors who do a special hike in Larch Valley near Lake Louise year after year. In fact, for some it's almost like making a pilgrimage because of the outstanding weather and beauty.

Fossils Within Yoho National Park is one of the most significant and richest finds of fossils on planet earth. The fossils of the Burgess Shale have expanded scientific understanding of the evolution of animal life. They are nicely interpreted at the Yoho Visitor Centre.

Yoho National Park is also known for its two scenic waterfalls. The Takakkaw Falls, which is in the northeast section of Yoho National Park and close to the Continental Divide, begins at Daly Glacier and flows into the Yoho River which flows into Kicking Horse River which flows into Columbia River at Golden, British Columbia.

Wapta Falls, which is located in the southwest section of Yoho National Park, is the full width of the Kicking Horse River and drops about 100 feet. It is a spectacular view.

Guided tours to the Burgess Shales fossil beds are available through the Yoho Burgess Shale Foundation. Avid hikers from Germany come regularly to the Rockies in the fall of the year. They love the Rockies because of the sense of space and high mountains.

Banff is a fall flyway for Golden Eagles. Visitors can sometimes view numerous eagles flying south over a period of weeks. Two of the best viewing places are the Vermilion Lakes and Lake Minnewanka. The nearby town of Canmore, Alberta celebrates the event with the Festival of Eagles. In the spring, visitors also have an opportunity to see the Golden Eagles flying north.

The Festival for Mountain Films is another popular fall activity. Each year for the past ten years the Festival has been held at the Banff Centre for the Performing Arts. Films from around the world that celebrate mountain living in one fashion or another are shown. Other fall events include a Mountain Book Festival and an International Television Festival.

Winters are truly a wonderland in Canada's Mountain Parks. Ski resorts in Banff and Jasper provide some of the best skiing in the world. In Banff National Park, for example, there is Mount Norquay, Sunshine Village, and Lake Louise Ski Resort while in Jasper there is Marmot Basin.

Skiing starts as early as November 10th and often goes to mid May. Should one arrive at the mountains without skis, they can be rented.

At Ski Banff-Lake Louise, there is a tri-area ski program. In other words, an individual or family can have the opportunity to ski three separate and distinct ski resorts which includes more than 7,000 acres of skiing terrain.

The program also includes a tri-area pass which gives access to all three ski resorts any day of the week. The pass includes transportation to and from one's hotel. The program features the opportunity for the skier to decide which one of the ski resorts he or she would like to ski daily, be it Banff Mount Norquay or Sunshine Village or Lake Louise Ski Resort.

The primary benefit of skiing in the four Mountain National Parks is that the visitor can ski in a wilderness area where the slopes are devoid of condominiums.

The snow is also world famous. Snow is drier in the Rockies. Once the temperature reaches a certain low, it stays low, and as a result, there is an absence of melting-freezing throughout the winter. Because the temperature stays colder, the snow ends up being a lot softer and easier, too. Thus, if a skier is looking for powder skiing, this is certainly the area for it.

As well as programs for the advanced skier, each of the four ski resorts offer beginner programs for those who want to take up skiing for the very first time.

Cross-country skiing is also a very popular winter activity. Visitors ski across frozen lakes and through forests and glades following clearly marked trails and using maps which are available from each of the Park information offices.

There are more than 80 miles of track-set cross-country ski trails in Banff National Park, and some of the trails can be accessed right from the community of Banff. Equipment can also be readily rented from local stores.

Jasper National Park, the furthest north of the four National Parks, is also a great place to go cross country skiing in the wintertime and enjoy watching wildlife: coyotes, elk, moose, and wolves.

Still another winter pastime is for visitors to take the sleigh rides which are offered in both Banff and Lake Louise. At Banff, the ride takes one over the top of the Bow River. At Lake Louise, the ride circumvents the lake. The sleigh ride drivers also provide interpretation on flora and fauna.

Other winter opportunities include dog sled rides, ice fishing, ice-skating, snow shoeing, and trail rides. At both the Fairmont Jasper Park Lodge and Fairmont Chateau Lake Louise, one can skate on frozen lakes adjacent to the hotels. Skates can be rented from a concessionaire at the hotels and from several shops in the hamlet of Lake Louise or the town of Jasper.

At Christmas time, in particular, with music playing in the background, the setting is just gorgeous. There is also an indoor skating rink at the Recreation Center on Norquay Road in the Town of Banff.

There is also the opportunity to take a neat canyon hike through spectacular Maligne Canyon over the frozen Maligne River. In the wintertime, an ice walk is also offered at Johnston Canyon.

In both cases, the hikers put on crampons in order to avoid slipping on the ice as the visitor

hikes up the trails, and a naturalist explains the natural surroundings. Winter views in this area are incredible because everything is frozen and pristine.

There are also opportunities for snowmobiling. However, because snowmobiling is not allowed within the Parks, concessionaires take snowmobilers to an area close to Golden, B.C. The concessionaire supplies all that is needed, and the typical program includes lunch and transportation.

Snowshoeing programs are also popular. The local guides will take the snowshoers to different parts of the Parks depending upon the weather, temperature, snow conditions and what the snowshoers want to see. The groups are kept small and led by guides who will pick up the snowshoers in the morning, supply all the equipment, and return the snowshoers back to their hotel/motel at the close of the day. Today's snowshoes, made of high-tech, carbide-graphite, weigh very little. Snowshoeing has proven to be a wonderful family activity.

During the winter, visitors can also learn to ice climb at the mountainous end of Lake Louise. Information on that program is available through Chateau Lake Louise or through the Information Centre in Lake Louise hamlet.

For more than 80 years, the Banff Winter Festival has annually featured ten days of winter fun for visitors of all ages with 30 other events from the Snow Ambassador Contest to the Wine Challenge.

Also, Ice Magic, an annual international ice carving competition, is held in Lake Louise during the middle of January.

Banff itself is a unique example of an international resort located within a National Park. Also what is unique about Banff is the cultural life of that community.

Take, for example, the Whyte Museum of the Canadian Rockies, which chronicles the history of the European peoples who settled in the Canadian Rockies, including some of the first Park wardens, artists, and painters who came to the Mountain Parks.

The Cave and Basin National Historic Site commemorates the birthplace of Banff National Park. Interpretive exhibits, videos, and self-guiding trails tell the story of the discovery of Banff's hot springs. The Banff Park Museum is western Canada's oldest natural history museum, with wildlife specimens dating back to the 1860's.

Finally, the Cascade Gardens located behind the Banff National Park Administration Building, features fragrant flowers, ponds, and cascading waterfalls.

Banff is also home to the Banff Centre for the Performing Arts. Depending upon what is offered on a given day, the visitor to Banff, as well as local residents, can enjoy international caliber opera and theater, plus arts, crafts, and lectures.

Concluding, a recent survey of visitors representing 12 countries, 25 states, and 6 provinces indicated the major reasons for their enjoyment of the Canadian Rockies were the physical beauty of the area, the friendliness of the people, and the wide range of activities available.

Is it any wonder all four Mountain Parks of the Canadian Rockies make up part of a World Heritage Site designated by the United Nations because of the cultural, historical, and natural significance of the area!

A Heritage Tourism Strategy has been put in place by Parks Canada, the business community, and various stakeholders who are interested in the Parks and want to work together to promote the Canadian Rockies in the proper manner.

Also of interest, east of Banff National Park and southeast of Calgary, is Dinosaur Provincial Park and the fifty million dollar Royal Tyrrell Museum of Paleontology. This museum is also a World Heritage Site and worthy of a visit by those visiting the Canadian Rockies. Are you making plans for a vacation? Try the Canadian Rockies. You'll be glad you did.

Editorial Note: The Canadian Rocky Mountain National Parks include Banff, Jasper, Yoho, and Kootenay. However, because tourists traveling between Calgary and Vancouver on Trans Canada Highway 1 usually also visit Mount Revelstoke National Park and Glacier National Park of Canada, I have included these Parks on the map on page 17.

If after reading our color picture book, you would like to do additional reading about the Canadian Rocky Mountain National Parks, the following books are available:

Canadian Rocky Mountain National Parks

GUIDES & HANDBOOKS

Banff: History Attractions, Activities: An Altitude Superguide
by Sebastian Hutchings

Banff National Park and the Canadian Rockies For Dummies 2nd Edition
by Darlene West

Banff-Jasper Explorers Guide
by Carl Schreier, Raymond Gehman

Canadian Rockies - An Altitude SuperGuide
by Graeme Pole

Field Guide to Banff National Park
Field Naturalist

Frommer's Banff and Jasper National Parks
by Christie Pashby

Handbook of the Canadian Rockies
by Ben Gadd

Lonely Planet Banff, Jasper & Glacier National Parks
by Korina Miller, Susan Derby, David Lukas

Moon Handbooks Canadian Rockies: Including Banff and Jasper National Parks

by Andrew Hempstead

Biking in the Rockies
Backcountry Biking in the Canadian Rockies - New Edition (2003)

by Doug Eastcott

Ice Climbing in the Rockies
Mixed Climbs in the Canadian Rockies - 2nd Edition

by Sean Isaac

Rock Climbing
Bouldering in the Canadian Rockies

by Fink, Norman & Tremaine

Mountaineering
Mountaineering - The Freedom of the Hills

Edited by Graydon & Hanson
By Christopher Van Tilburg

HIKING BOOKS & MAPS

Backcountry Banff
by Mike Potter

Banff's Best Day Hikes
by Heather Elton

The Canadian Rockies Trail Guide- 7th Edition
by Brian Patton & Bart Robinson

Classic Hikes in the Canadian Rockies - Revised 2005
by Graeme Pole

The David Thompson Highway: A Hiking Guide
by Jane Ross & Daniel Kyba

**Don't Waste Your Time in the Canadian Rockies:
The Opinionated Hiking Guide**
by Kathy Copeland, Craig Copeland

Fire Lookout Hikes in the Canadian Rockies
by Mike Potter

Hiking Canada's Great Divide Trail
by Dustin Lynx

Hiking Lake Louise - New Edition
by Mike Potter

Hiking Rocky Mountain National Park, 9th
by Kent Dannen, Donna Dannen

Hiking Yoho, Kootenay, Glacier & Mt. Revelstoke National Parks
by Michelle Gurney, Kathy Howe

Ridgewalks in the Canadian Rockies
by Mike Potter

Rocky Mountain National Park Dayhiker's Guide: A Scenic Guide to 33 Favorite Hikes Including Longs Peak
by Jerome Malitz

Rocky Mountain National Park: The Complete Hiking Guide
by Lisa Foster

Scrambles in the Canadian Rockies - New Edition (2003)
by Alan Kane

Walks and Easy Hikes
by Graeme Pole

MAPS:

Banff, Kootenay & Yoho National Parks
1:200 000 Topographical Maps

Banff Up Close
1:35 000 - A Gemtrek Map

Banff National Park Map by ITMB (Map)
by International Travel Maps and Books

Banff & Mount Assiniboine
1:100 000 - A Gemtrek Map

Banff, Kootenay & Yoho National Parks
1:200 000 - Topographical Map

Best of Lake Louise
1:35 000 - A Gemtrek Map

Best of Jasper
1:35 000 - A Gemtrek Map

Jasper National Park Map (Travel Reference Map S.)
by International Travel Maps

Jasper & Maligne Lake
1:100 000 - A Gemtrek Map

Jasper National Park
1:200 000 - Topographical Map

Kootenay National Park

1:100 000 - A Gemtrek Map

Lake Louise & Yoho
1:50 000 - A Gemtrek Map

PHOTOS / PHOTOGRAPHY

Banff National Park: A Pictorial Guide
by Graeme Wallace

The Canadian Rockies
by Douglas Leighton (Photographer)

Canadian Rockies Photo Album
by Elizabeth Wilson

Dances With Light: Photographs Of The Canadian Rockies
By Darwin Wiggett
by Darwin Wiggett

The Great Divide: Photographs from the Canadian Rockies
by Ernie Kroeger

High Above the Canadian Rockies: Spectacular Aerial Photography
by Russ Heinl

How To Photograph The Canadian Rockies
by Darwin Wiggett

John Shaw's Nature Photography Field Guide
by John Shaw

Lonely Planet Wildlife Travel Photography: A Guide to Taking Better Pictures
by Andy Rouse

National Audubon Guide to Nature Photography
by Tim Fitzharris

Photographing Wildlife in the Canadian Rockies
by Dennis & Esther Schmidt

Portrait of the Canadian Rockies
by Bela Baliko

HISTORY - BIOGRAPHY

Lake Louise at it's Best : An affectionate look at life at Lake Louise by one who knew it well
by Roger Patillo

Switchbacks: True Stories from the Canadian Rockies Men for the Mountains
by Sid Marty

Yoho: A History And Celebration of Yoho National Park
by R. J. Sandford

NATURE

The Crucible of Creation: The Burgess Shale and the Rise of Animals
by Simon Conway-Morris

How Old Is That Mountain?: A Visitor's Guide to the Geology of Banff And Yoho National Parks
by Chris Yorath

Of Rocks, Mountains and Jasper: Exploring the Geology of Jasper National Park
by Chris Yorath, Ben Gadd

Rocky Mountain Natural History: Grand Teton to Jasper
by Daniel Mathews

Scats and Tracks of the Rocky Mountains, 2nd
by James Halfpenny

Wonderful Life: The Burgess Shale and the Nature of History (Paperback)
by Stephen Jay Gould

COOKBOOK

A Taste of the Canadian Rockies
by Myriam Leighton & Chip Olver (Editors)

KIDS BOOKS: Picture Books & Chapter Books

Bears
by Deborah Hodge

Beavers
by Deborah Hodge, Pat Stephens

Deer, Moose, Elk & Caribou

by Deborah Hodge

Little Beaver and The Echo

by Amy MacDonald, Sarah Fox-Davies

Eagles

by Deborah Hodge, Nancy Gray Ogle

C is for Chinook

by Dawn Welykochy

Emily Carr: At the Edge of the World

by Jo Ellen Bogart, Maxwell Newhouse

Glaciers (First Books Series)

by Roy A. Gallantw

Salmon Forest

by David Suzuki, Sarah Ellis, Sheena Lott

Printed in the United States
By Bookmasters